I0014470

Hacking University Senior Edition

Linux

Optimal beginner's guide to precisely learn and conquer the Linux operating system. A complete step-by-step guide in how the Linux command line works

BY ISAAC D. CODY

HACKING UNIVERSITY

SENIOR EDITION

LINUX

Optimal Beginner's Guide To Precisely Learn And
Conquer The Linux Operating System. A Complete Step
By Step Guide In How Linux Command Line Works

ISAAC D. CODY

Table of Contents

More Linux Information

What Next and Conclusion

responsibility or blame be held against the publisher for any reparation, damages, or monetary loss due to the information herein, either directly or indirectly.

Respective authors own all copyrights not held by the publisher.

The information herein is offered for informational purposes solely, and is universal as so. The presentation of the information is without contract or any type of guarantee assurance.

The trademarks that are used are without any consent, and the publication of the trademark is without permission or backing by the trademark owner. All trademarks and brands within this book are for clarifying purposes only and are the owned by the owners themselves, not affiliated with this document.

Disclaimer

Introduction

Computers contain two functional components- software and hardware. The hardware is the physical parts that spin, compute, and use electricity to perform calculations, but software is a more virtual concept. Essentially, software consists of programming code that gives instructions to the hardware- telling the parts what to do. There is "high level" software such as Internet browsers, word processors, music players, and more. But the often overlooked component is the "low level" software known as an operating system.

Operating systems are required for our personal computers to work. At an office, or with a relatively inexpensive desktop computer the operating system used is probably Microsoft's Windows. Content creators, writers, and graphic artists prefer Apple computers because they come with the creativity-focused OSX operating system.

Those two OS's, Windows and OSX, have dominated the consumer market for many years. However, an alternative operating system exists that excels in usability, customization, security, and price. OS's based off of the relatively unknown Linux meet and exceed in all of those areas, but it remains an obscure option that many people have not even heard of.

Linux is not an operating system by itself. It is a kernel, or the "core" of an OS. Just as Windows NT is the kernel of Windows 7, Linux is the kernel of "distributions" such as Ubuntu, Debian, Arch, Fedora, and more.

But why would anybody abandon the familiarity of Windows for an unheard of computing environment? Linux is not only monetarily free, but it is also compatible with a huge range of devices. Older computers, and especially ones that no longer work can be rejuvenated with a Linux OS, making it run as though it were new again.

This book will explicate upon the benefits of switching to Linux, as well as serve as a beginners guide to installing, configuring, and using the most popular distribution. Then, the terminal command line will be explained to tell how to take advantage of the OS in ways not possible in other systems. Truly there are many advantages to be gained by switching to Linux, and you just might find a suitable primary OS to use on your computers by reading this book.

History of Linux

In the early 1990s Linus Torvalds was a student in Finland. Computers of the time usually ran on either DOS or UNIX, two operating systems that were both proprietary and difficult to use at the time. Torvalds sought to create his own operating system as a hobby project (based off of UNIX), but the project quickly grew and attracted more developers. The kernel continued to transform until it was portable (usable on a variety of systems) and entirely usable for computing. A kernel is not an OS, though, so Linux was combined with the GNU core utilities to create a computing environment reminiscent of an operating system.

Then, 3rd party organizations took the base Linux product and added their own high level software and features to it, thereby creating Linux "distributions". Linux remains a free hobby project even through today, and thus the kernel is continuously receiving updates and revisions by Torvalds and the community. Throughout the 2000s, many other 3rd parties saw the usefulness of the Linux environment and they began to incorporate it into their production environments and corporations. Today, Linux is known for being highly used in servers and business settings with a small dedicated desktop following. Working towards the future, the kernel has reached a level of popularity where it will never die out. Large companies revel in Linux because of its advantages and usefulness, and so the kernel and various distributions will always exist as the best alternative operating system.

Benefits of Linux

To compare how great of an option Linux is for a computer, we shall compare it to the more familiar modern operating systems.

First, Linux is free. The background of GNU places Linux into a "free and open source" mentality where most (if not all) of the software shipping with Linux is free. Free and open source (FOSS) refers to two things- the software is both monetarily free and the source code is also transparent. FOSS differs from proprietary software in that everything is open with FOSS, and there are no hidden spyware, fees, or catches involved with using it. The software is often more secure because anybody can contribute to the readily available source code and make it better. Because Linux and most of the software you can download for it is free, it is a fantastic operating system for small businesses or individual users on a budget. Certainly no quality is sacrificed by not charging a fee, because the Linux project and its various distributions are community-driven and funded through donations. Compare this to the cost of Windows, which is often many hundreds of dollars for the OS alone. Microsoft Office is a popular document writing program suite, but it also prices high. Free alternatives to these programs exist in Linux, and they definitely compare in quality to the big name products.

Probably the largest complaint held by PC owners is viruses. Windows computers are especially susceptible to them, and even anti-virus software companies are always playing catch-up to the newest threats. Simply visiting a malicious website is often enough to infect a computer, and many users choose Mac computers because of the significantly less frequency of incidents relating to malware. Linux-based operating systems are similar to Macs in that viruses are virtually non-existent. This increased security makes switching to Linux a must for anybody concerned about privacy, security, or reliability.

Linux is very popular within corporations and government agencies. This is because high-powered servers and critical devices will run remarkably better with Linux as the operating system. The OS is known for reliability and stability too. While a Windows computer will need regular restarts and maintenance to "freshen" it up and keep it from running slow, Linux servers can run months or even years without a single restart. IT professionals inevitably choose Linux to be the backbone of their network because of its reputation. Its renowned stability is available to consumers as well on the desktop platform, and it is definitely useful for us as well.

Perhaps the best benefit to using Linux is the speed. Low system requirements mean that computers that are normally slow and groggy on Windows will be zippy and quick on Linux. Users frustrated with computer slowdowns can replace their OS for a more responsive experience. Furthermore, Linux can be installed on older computers to reinvigorate them. So even though that old laptop may be too outdated for the newest version of Windows, there will probably be a distribution of Linux that will squeeze a few more years of useful life out of it.

Customization is a sought after feature in technology. Windows, and especially OSX, limit the amount that you can do with your operating system out of fear that the average user would break it. This is not the case with Linux, as it encourages editing and changing visuals and functionality of the OS. Of course it is not necessary, and the default configuration of most Linux distributions is extremely stable and difficult to break unintentionally. But for those that love jailbreaking, modding, and playing around with computers, Linux can facilitate the creative side and even provide curious hackers with access to tools unavailable in other systems.

And finally, Linux is compatible with a huge range of devices. Linux can run on almost any architecture, meaning it can be installed on cell phones, desktops, laptops, servers, game consoles, and "smart" devices. Hobbyists take pleasure in simply installing Linux on niche, old, or quirky devices simply because they can. For the average user, it means that Linux is probably compatible with your computer.

Overall, Linux beats out the mainstream operating systems in many areas. All of these things definitely make Linux the better choice for your computer, and you should use it to gain access to these revered features. Artists, hackers, creative individuals, small business owners, techies, non-techies, and just about everyone can find something to like about Linux. The wide range of distributions means there is something for everyone, so install Linux today to see what you can gain from it.

Linux Distributions

Installing Linux can be done in a few ways, such as burning an image of the OS onto a disc, writing it to a USB, ordering a Live CD from online, formatting an SD card, or trying one out via Virtual Box. Ultimately though you cannot just install "Linux" and have a usable OS. Because Linux is just the kernel, you will need the other software as well that gives you graphical user interfaces, Internet access, etc... As previously mentioned, "distributions" of Linux exist. Distributions are versions of Linux containing preinstalled programs and a distinctive style and focus. A distribution takes the core of Linux and makes it into an entire operating system fit for daily use.

There are a mind-boggling amount of distributions. Some have specific purposes, such as Kali Linux for hacking, Sugar Linux for education, or Arch Linux for customization. Others are more general purpose, such as Ubuntu and Debian. Getting the most out of installing Linux means you will need to understand about different distributions and make a choice as to which will work best for you. Read the following sections to understand what a few of the most popular distributions are used for.

Ubuntu is the most widely known distribution at the time of writing. Throughout the 2000's it gained popularity for being user friendly and intuitive. Based off of the earlier Debian distro, Ubuntu is very similar to Windows computers in use, meaning it is an excellent choice for the Linux newbie. Because of this, we will be installing an Ubuntu variant later in the book. Canonical Ltd is the company that actively develops Ubuntu- yearly versions updates mean that the OS is always up to date and usable with emerging technology. Despite this, Ubuntu still work on many older devices at a reasonable speed. Applications can be installed from a "store" of sorts, meaning that the beginning user does not need to understand the often complicated command line. Conclusively, the Ubuntu distro is a great choice for the first time Linux user, and you should install it to learn how Linux works without diving into the harder distros.

For more specific cases of computing, Ubuntu has various sub-distributions or "flavors". These are distros that use Ubuntu as a base but have a different focus, such as Lubuntu's emphasis on lightweight applications. Here are a few:

- Lubuntu – A version of Ubuntu designed to run on older hardware or computers with limited resources. The install file is less than 1GB, and the hardware requirements are much lower than standard Ubuntu. Use this distro for revitalizing older computers but while retaining the usability of Ubuntu.

- Ubuntu Studio – Ubuntu for artists including digital painters, sound producers, and video editors. Ubuntu studio is Ubuntu but with editing tools installed already.

- Kubuntu – Ubuntu reskinned with the KDE desktop environment. The look and feel of Kubuntu differs from the classic Ubuntu feel by providing a desktop environment that is more traditional to other operating systems.

- Xubuntu is another lightweight distro that is not as quite as bare bones as Lubuntu. Xubuntu sacrifices size and hardware requirements to provide an OS that works on old, but not too old computers. It certainly is more aesthetic than other minimal Linux distributions, and it also uses Ubuntu as a base for user-friendliness and familiarity.

- Ubuntu Server – A Ubuntu variant more suited to industrial and corporate needs,

Ubuntu server can be run headless and provide functionality for other Linux systems in a network.

- Mythbuntu – A variant with TV streaming and live television programs preinstalled. This is a great distro for converting old computers into "smart TV" devices via Kodi.

In conclusion, the wide range of Ubuntu distributions mean that there is a beginner OS for everybody. It is highly recommended that you take advantage of the ease of use features and general familiarity contained within Ubuntu. It serves as a stepping stone OS, one that will gradually introduce you to Linux. Definitely install it as your first Linux experience.

Linux Mint is a highly used OS in the Linux world. "Powerful and easy to use", Mint contains FOSS and proprietary software as well with the purpose of being a complete experience for Linux beginners. While not totally Linux-like, Mint is an excellent choice for a first-time alternate operating system. It consistently ranks among the most used operating systems ever, and its default layout is very similar to Windows facilitating a smooth transition into the Linux world.

Debian is one of the oldest Linux distributions, being created in 1993. Combining with the Linux philosophy, Debian keeps stability and solidity as the guiding development principal. Certainly the amount of time Debian has been around is an indicator of refinement, so those seeking an experience free of bugs and glitches can turn to Debian. Free and open source software also has a home in Debian, because most of the software contained within is FOSS. This does not mean that you are limited, though, because there is an official repository of non-free software for proprietary programs such as Adobe Flash. Debian is a decent choice for beginners, but Ubuntu still stands as the best introductory OS. Install Debian for stability, FOSS, and a wholly Linux experience.

Slackware is an OS that goes back even further than Debian. It stays close to the original Linux intent, meaning that you will have to install your own GUI and program dependencies. Because of that fact, Slackware is mostly for intermediate Linux users, as beginners will be confused at the unfamiliar methods. However, if you want to experience a Linux distribution that is closer to the UNIX roots, Slackware can provide for you.

Fedora is an OS more oriented towards workstations and business uses. Even Linus Torvalds himself is a user of Fedora, attributing to the operating system's popularity and use. Fedora is updated very often, meaning that it is always up-to-date and on the cutting edge of Linux technology. Security and FOSS are also a focus within the OS, which is why it is commonly used on endpoint computers in small businesses.

There could be a challenge with working with Fedora, though, so consider it as an intermediate OS.

Arch Linux is another distribution, but one that is mostly designed for experienced users. The OS comes as a shell of a system that the user can customize to their liking, by adding only the programs and services that they want. Because of this, Arch is difficult to set up, but a rewarding and learning experience as well. By building your own personal system, you will understand the deeper Linux concepts that are hidden from you on the higher level distributions. Install this advanced OS after becoming very comfortable with the basics.

And finally, there is an abundance of other unique distributions that are worth mentioning. In the following list, we will talk about a few of them. Just note that there are so many distributions, this entire book could be filled describing each and every niche use.

- CrunchBang – A Debian-based distribution that aims to be less resource intensive. It is simple and without some of the bloatware that some distributions include by default. CrunchBang can run fast and be efficient at computing.

- Android – The popular phone OS is actually a Linux variant. Since many phones have lower specifications than full desktop PCs, the OS is a great choice for laptops, touchscreen devices, or home media computers. Furthermore, you can use many of the Google Apps from the Play store, meaning that thousands of apps, games, and utilities are available to be used on your phone and computer. While it is not recommended as your first Linux OS, it is definitely a neat choice for experimenting with older computers or children's PCs.

- Chrome OS – Another mobile-type OS developed by Google, Chrome OS is essentially a lightweight Linux browser meant for online use. Google has this OS preinstalled on their ChromeBooks, which have lower specifications than other laptops. But the OS is really only a full screen Chrome browser, so the OS is perfect for users wanting an uncomplicated experience or a dedicated Internet machine.

- Tiny Core – An OS measured in megabytes, Tiny Core is for antique computers or embedded devices. This OS is mostly for intermediate users that have a hobby project or dedicated purpose in mind.

- Damn Small Linux – Another minimal Linux variant, this OS is best for quick access to a Linux command line.

- openSUSE – This is a distribution for experienced computer users. With many tools for administrators and program developers, openSUSE is the best OS for users confident in their skills.

Positively the number of operating systems based off of the Linux kernel is astounding. With a huge amount of choices, you might be confused as to where to start and how to install it. When in doubt (and as we will demonstrate shortly), install Ubuntu or one of its variants. The OS is great for beginners and makes the Linux transition smoother. But as you increase in skill and wish to learn more about Linux, you can always install another operating system.

Booting Into Linux

If you are ready to take the plunge into a Linux based distribution, the first thing you must do is back up your files. Overwriting the OS on your hard drive will erase any data contained within, meaning you must back up any pictures, music, or files you wish to keep after the transition. Use an external hard drive, or an online data storage site (such as Google Drive) to temporarily hold your files. We are not responsible for you losing something important, back it up!

Next we will need to choose an OS. This book will use Ubuntu 16.04 as an extended example, and it is recommended you do the same. Navigate to Canonical's official website (http://www.ubuntu.com) and acquire a copy of the OS. You will download the image from the site to your computer.

Next we need to obtain an installation media. This can be a DVD, a USB drive, an SD card, or any other writable media that your computer can read. The only restriction is that the device must be able to hold an image as large as the OS download, so 4GB should be suffice. Remove everything from the drive, as it will also be formatted.

Download a tool for writing the image file. For DVDs install Imgburn (http://www.imgburn.com/), and for flash media download Rufus (https://rufus.akeo.ie/). The most common method of OS installation is to use a 4GB USB drive, and it is more recommended. Insert your media, start the appropriate program, select the OS image that was downloaded, and begin the writing process. It will take some time, as the image needs to be made bootable on the media. When it is finished, you can shut down your computer fully.

This is the point to make double sure you are ready to install Linux. Check that your files are backed up, understand that you will be erasing your current OS, and preferably have a Windows/OSX install disc handy in case you decide to switch back. If you are indeed ready to switch, continue.

With the installation media still inserted, turn on your computer. The first screen that you will see is the BIOS / UEFI POST screen, and it will give a keyboard button that you should press to enter setup. This screen shows every time you boot, but you probably pay no attention to it. Press the indicated key to enter the BIOS setup. If you are too slow, the screen will disappear and your usual OS will begin to load. If this happens, simply shut the computer back down and try again.

Once within the BIOS / UEFI, you will have to navigate to the "boot order" settings. Every computer's BIOS / UEFI is slightly different, so we cannot explain the process in detail. But generally you can follow button prompts at the bottom of the screen to understand how to navigate. After arriving at the boot order settings, place your boot medium at the top of the list. As an example, if you used a USB drive, then you would see its name and have to bring it to the top of the list. These settings control the order in which the PC searches for operating systems. With our boot medium at the top of the list, it will boot into our downloaded Linux image instead of our usual OS. Save your settings and restart the computer. If everything was done correctly the computer will begin to boot into Ubuntu.

But if something goes wrong, try troubleshooting it with these tips:

- Primary OS boots instead of Linux –
  You probably did not save the settings
  with your alternate boot medium at the

top of the list. The PC is still defaulting to the internal HDD to boot.

- "No boot media found" – Did you "drag and drop" your Linux image onto the media instead of writing it? Without explicitly telling the computer it is bootable, it will not know what to do with the data files on the media. Alternatively, you could have a corrupted download, or an incomplete write. Try downloading the image again and making another installation.

- "Kernel Panic" – Something is wrong with the boot process. See above for the possibility of a corrupted installation. Otherwise, the image you are trying to install may not be compatible with your hardware. IF you see any other error messages, do an Internet search on them. For prebuilt computers and laptops, search for the model name and Linux to find other user's experiences.

Finally, you might have attempted to install a 64-bit image on a 32-bit computer. With your next image download, specifically select a 32-bit image.

- "Problem reading data from CD-ROM..." – Try using a different install medium, because some distributions no longer support CD and DVD installations. USB drives are recommended.

- PC seems to boot, but there is nothing at all on the screen – If you are using a dedicated graphics card (compared to integrated GFX from the CPU), Linux might not be recognizing it completely. Plug your monitor into the motherboard directly instead of the card.

But most of those problems are rare or simply due to user error. Linux has high compatibility and is relatively easy to install/use past the initial installation. The typical user will have Ubuntu boot successfully at this point, and they will be presented with a working computing environment.

The desktop you see is referred to as a "Live CD", which is pretty much a demonstration of the OS and how it works. You have not actually installed the OS to your hard drive yet, as it is still running directly from your boot media. It is a chance for you to test out Linux without actually removing your primary OS, so take the opportunity to explore how Linux distributions work.

Ubuntu Basics

Similar to Windows, Ubuntu has a desktop graphical user interface. Applications open within Windows that can be maximized, minimized, closed, and moved around with the top bar. Ubuntu also has a "task bar" of sorts that functions much like its Windows counterpart- icons resemble programs that can be launched by clicking on them. The "Windows Button" (called the Dash Button) on the task bar is used to open a search functionality from which you can type in the name of a program or file on your computer to quickly start it.

Furthermore, there is a bar at the top of the screen that works like the "menu" bar of other operating systems. This is where drop-down menus such as "file", "edit", "help", etc... will appear once a program is active.

Besides a few nominal differences Ubuntu functions is a very familiar way. In fact, many of the programs that you may already use on other operating systems, such as Firefox, are available and sometimes preinstalled on Linux distributions. With enough experimentation and practice, you will be able to navigate the GUI of Ubuntu as if you were a professional. Continue exploring the system, and continue if you are ready to replace your main operating system with this Linux one.

Installing Linux

On the desktop, you will see an "Install Ubuntu 16.04 LTS" icon. Double clicking it will launch an application that makes installation very easy. If you are not connected to the Internet, do so now by plugging in an Ethernet cord or by connecting to Wi-Fi from the top right icon. Select your language and click "continue". The next prompt will ask whether you would like to download updates and install third-party software during the OS installation. These options are highly recommended for beginners, so check them and click "continue".

The application will move on to another screen asking for your install method. There are various options, such as erasing the disk altogether, installing alongside your primary OS, or updating a previous version of Linux. Select an option that works best for you. If you are still hesitant about making a full switch, elect to install Ubuntu as your secondary OS. That option will allow you to choose which OS to boot into after the BIOS screen. Nevertheless, select your option and click "install now".

While Ubuntu installs, you can specify a few other options, such as your time zone, computer name, account name, and password. The entire installation should not take too long, but it will take long enough that your computer should be plugged in (if it is a laptop). After finishing, the OS will require a reboot. Congratulations, you now have a usable Linux system on your computer. Throughout the next chapters in this publication we will focus on Linux concepts, how do achieve certain tasks, and how to further your knowledge of your system.

Managing Hardware and Software

Hardware in Linux is actually much easier to manage than hardware on Windows. Instead of downloading individual drivers for devices, most of the drivers are built-in to the OS itself. This means that most popular devices can simply be installed with no further steps involved before they are usable. Printers, networks, hard drives, and other common devices are included- fiddling with drivers is not usually needed on Linux.

However, powerful graphics cards and other specific hardware will need proprietary drivers from that company to function to full efficiency. Because although your graphics card works by default with Linux, the secret and often hidden technology within can only be fully utilized with that company's software. On Ubuntu the process is straightforward- open the "additional drivers" application and let the OS search for you. After determining whether you have the devices, it will ask you which version of the driver to use. Follow any on-screen prompts to enable the 3rd party drivers. For any devices that do not appear, do Internet research on the manufacturer's website to determine whether they released a specific Linux driver that you can download.

Software is another aspect of Linux that excels over Windows. Much like an Apple computer, Ubuntu has an app store of sorts from which you can search through repositories of applications that are compatible with your device to download and install with just a few clicks. Just search for the "Ubuntu Software Center" from dash to open the application. From there you can browse individual categories such as "Games", "Office", or "System" for a list of programs, or you can search directly by name. After finding a program, click on it and then queue up the download by clicking "install". After authenticating yourself the software will automatically download and install. From there, the application can be run by searching for it in the dash.

Another method of installing software is available through the terminal, but we will discuss that later. Ubuntu is not totally limited to software found in the app store, because programs downloaded from the Internet can also be installed. Once again, we will touch on that subject after discussing the terminal.

Overall, managing hardware and software in Ubuntu is effortless. Whether installing a new hardware device or downloading a popular program, Linux distributions make you're computing experience trouble-free. That is not to say that Linux is wholly meant for beginners, because as we will learn Linux is definitely a great choice for power users and experienced admins.

The Command Line / Terminal

Before modern computers, hardware and software were interfaced by using keyboards exclusively. The mouse brought graphical interfaces and simplified the process, but many functions remained text-only as to not present complicated options to end users. In Linux, this process continues today. There exists the GUI that is present on most distributions, but every Linux distro also has a built-in text-based interface as well, from which powerful commands can be typed and executed. Think of the terminal as a much more powerful command prompt, because you can completely use your computer exclusively through the terminal alone. With enough knowledge, a user can actually browse the Internet, install programs, manage their file system, and more through text.

Begin the terminal by launching it from dash or by using the Ctrl+Alt+T keyboard shortcut. A purple window will open and wait for your input. You can type a command and press enter to activate it. For our first command, enter "ls". This is short for list, and it will display all of the files within our current directory. You will be able to see the files and folders in Home, Ubuntu's main user folder. If you are lost, you can always type in "pwd" to print the working directory and display the name of the folder you are currently browsing. As you learn commands, it helps to write them down as to better internalize their use.

Managing Directories

       Directories, another name for folders, work the same as they do in other operating systems. Folders hold files, and you must be currently accessing a directory in order to interact with the files inside of it. You can use the terminal command "cd" to change directory and move about the file system. As an example, typing "cd Desktop" from the Home folder will transfer you to that folder. Now using "ls" will not show anything (unless you added files to the desktop). To back out, type "cd ..". Practice navigating around the file system in this fashion; cd into a directory and ls to view the files.

       Because you are typing commands, Linux expects your input to be exact. If you misspell a command it will simply not work, and if you type a folder or file incorrectly it will try to reference something that does not exist. Watch your input carefully when using the terminal.

Opening a file is done with a different command – ".". The period is used to start the specified file, so if you were attempting to open a picture it could be done like so: "./house.png". Both the period and the slash are necessary, as it denotes that you are running a file within the current directory. When you run a file it will be opened with the default application assigned to the file type, so in the case of a picture it will most likely be opened in an image viewer.

You can also create and remove directories and files through terminal as well. For this example navigate to the Home directory. As a shortcut you can type "cd ~" to change the directory to your Home, because the tilde key is short for "the current user's home". Make a directory with the "mkdir" command; type, "mkdir Programming" to create a new folder with that title. You can CD into it, or you can go to the GUI and enter it to prove that you have indeed created a new folder. Now remove that directory by going

Home and typing "rmdir Programming". Without hesitation, Linux will remove the specified directory. Similarly, using "rm" will remove the specified file.

Linux has a design philosophy that many users are not used to. In Windows and OSX, the OS will almost always double check that you want to commence with an action such as deleting a file or uninstalling a program. Linux distributions believe that if you are imitating an event, you definitely mean to follow through with it. It will not typically confirm deleting something, nor will it display any confirmation messages (file successfully deleted). Rather, the absence of a message indicates the process completed successfully. While the philosophy is somewhat dangerous (because you could potentially ruin your OS installation without warning), it serves as a design contrast to other operating systems. Linux gives you complete control, and it never tries to hide anything or obscure options because they might be too complicated. It takes some time to get used to, but most users agree it is a welcome change to be respected by the technology they own.

      This does not compromise security, however, because any critical action requires the "sudo" command as a preface. Sudo stands for "super user do", meaning that the user of the highest permissions is requesting the following command. Any sudo entry will require an administrator password, so malicious software or un-intending keyboard spammers cannot accidently do damage without knowing the password first. A lot of the commands we use in this book require sudo permissions, so if the command fails to complete with a message explaining it does not have enough permissions you can retry with sudo.

Apt

Learning the terminal opens up computer functions that are not available through the GUI. Also, you can shorten the amount of time it takes to do many things by typing it instead. Take, for instance, the amount of work required installing a program. If you wanted to download the Google Chromium browser, you would have to open the software center, type in the name of the program, locate the correct package, mark it for installation, and execute the action. Compare that to typing "sudo apt-get install chromium-browser" into the terminal. With that one command, Ubuntu will save you many minutes.

Apt (advanced packaging tool) is the command associated with managing applications in Ubuntu. Other distributions may use their own tool, but apt is commonly used for its large repositories and simple commands. Packages are installed with the "apt-get install" formatting, where you specify the name of the program you wish to install. In the example above we specify the Chromium program with the package name "chromium-browser". Given that you do not know every package name, there is another command "apt-cache search" that can be used to locate package names matching the supplied string. So "apt-cache search chromium" would show "chromium-browser", and you could specify the correct name to install.

The usefulness of apt extends beyond that, as you can use it to update every single application on your system with a few commands. Use "apt-get update" to refresh the repository, then use "apt-get upgrade" to have every application upgrade itself to the newest version. Windows OS users should be envious at this easy process, because updating a Windows programs requires uninstalling and reinstalling with the newest version.

As time goes by, you might need to update the Ubuntu version. Every year there is a new release, and it can be installed with "apt-get dist-upgrade". Staying up to date with the newest fixes and additions ensures your Linux system will be working healthy for a long time. You might have even noticed that installing and updating the system does not require a reboot; a feature that contributes to Linux computer's lengthy uptimes and stability. Lastly, removing an application is done with "apt-get remove" followed by the package name.

To run the programs that we install we can either search for them from the dash, or we can just type the package name into the terminal. Typing "chromium-browser" will launch it just the same as double clicking its icon would. Some programs must be started from the command line by typing the package name exclusively because the package does not show up in a dash search. Overall utilizing the terminal is a time-saver and a great way to practice moving away from slow and cumbersome graphical user interfaces.

Easy installation and management of packages is a Linux feature that becomes highly useful- master it to improve your experience. There is a third method of installing packages, and it involves downloading and launching .deb files from the Internet. Some software are bundled in that format, and they act similar to .exe files in that they just need to be double clicked to begin the installation process.

More Terminal Commands

Here are a few more basic terminal commands that you should internalize and put to use in your system. Fully understanding the basics will provide a decent foundation upon which to build on later.

- cp – "cp image1.jpg image2.jpg" – copies (and renames) the first parameter to the second supplied parameter. Copy directories with the –r switch.

- mv – "mv cat.jpg /home/Pictures" – Move the specified file to the given directory.

- shutdown – "shutdown –h now" – shuts down the computer. –h is a tag meaning "halt", but you can also use –r to restart. Now refers to the time until it executes.

- date – "date" – Displays the current date and time.

- free – "free –g" – Show the current RAM usage of programs.

- du – "du –h" – Give the HDD usage.

- ps – "ps" – Show the active processes using CPU time.

- touch – "touch memo.txt" – Used to create a new blank file in the current directory with the specified name.

- ifconfig – "ifconfig" – The Linux equivalent of ipconfig, it shows network information.

Some commands have "tags" or "switches" associated with them. These are the letters preceded by dashes. They all do different things, and learning which switches to use for what purpose is best found through that command's manual pages. See the advanced section for opening the manual.

One of the most useful programs from the command line, nano is a simple text editor that can be used to edit files and quickly make changes to settings or scripts. It is accessed by typing "nano" into a command line. You can type a file as needed and then press ctrl+x to save and quit. As you save, you will give it the name and file extension associated with it; notes.txt will create a text file with the name "notes". Alternatively, you can edit a file by typing "nano notes.txt". In that example, we open notes in the editor and display its contents in an editable state.

Nano may be very simple, but it is undoubtedly powerful and a time saver for quick changes and file creation.

Connecting to Windows / Mac Computers

Windows and OSX computers have built-in networking functions such as workgroups, domains, shares, and more. Integrating Linux computers into the network infrastructure that has been dominated by Windows server computers is fairly easy, though, and correct setup will allow you to see Windows shares as well as join corporate domains.

The first step to intercommunication is installing the "samba" package. Either find it through the software center, or type in "sudo apt-get install samba" to obtain and install the necessary software.

Sharing files from your Ubuntu machine to other computers involves creating a samba share. Samba runs off of the same protocols that other popular file sharing methods use, so files shared from the Ubuntu machine can easily be seen on Windows. After installing samba, use "sudo nano /etc/samba/smb.conf" to start editing the configuration file. At the very bottom of the file add these lines:

[share]

comment = File Share from Ubuntu

path = /srv/samba/share

browsable = yes

guest ok = yes

read only = no

create mask = 0755

Now, create the folder specified in
"path" (sudo mkdir -p /srv/samba/share) and
set permissions (sudo chown nobody:nogroup
/srv/samba/share/) so that anybody can
access its contents. Place any files you want to
share within that directory, and then restart
the service (sudo restart smbd, sudo restart
nmbd) to make the share active. Lastly, log on
to your other computer and navigate to the
network shares. In Windows, they will appear
in the left panel of file explorer. If the share
does not appear automatically, type the IP
into the file path box (find Ubuntu IP with
ifconfig). You are now able to access Ubuntu's
files from other operating systems.

You might also need to see files from other operating systems in the Ubuntu computer. Firstly, open the Ubuntu file explorer. From the menu bar, click "files", and then select "connect to server". In the resulting box, type the URL of the share you wish to access. It could be an ftp address (ftp://ftp.test.com), an http address (http://test.com), or a share address (smb://share/Folder). Without any additional hardware or setup, you can see the files this way.

Finally, joining a domain such as Active Directory allows your computer to interact with other operating systems on the network and achieve other business-oriented tasks. Whether you have a small home network, or whether you are adding Linux computers to a corporate domain, the process is the same. Install a few extra packages (realmd, sssd, sssd-tools, samba-common, samba-common-bin, samba-libs, krb5-user, adcli, packagekit). While installing them, it will ask for your domain name. Enter it in all caps. Enter "kinit -V adminname" replacing that with an actual admin account name in the domain.

After entering the password you will have been authenticated to the domain. Now joining it is done with "realm --verbose join -U adminmame domainname.loc".

If it fails, it means the DNS is misconfigured on our device. Type "echo 'ad_hostname = nix01.domainname.loc' >> /etc/sssd/sssd.conf", then "echo 'dyndns_update = True' >> /etc/sssd/sssd.conf" and finally use "service sssd restart" to restart with those new settings. The first line sets the FQDN of our computer, so the line needs to be changed according to our domain settings. After a successful restart with correctly configured settings the terminal will claim it has joined the domain. Test this with "realm list". Now connected to AD you can administer the Linux device from your server!

For most users, however, creating shares and joining domains is far beyond the connectivity needs. Simple file sharing is much better done through USB drive transfers or a service such as Dropbox. Indeed Dropbox can be installed on the big three operating systems and files can be synced between them with no additional setup. On Ubuntu either download the .deb file directly from the website, install it from the software center, or use "sudo apt-get install nautilus-dropbox" to obtain the application. Within the Dropbox folder, place any files that you wish to transfer between computers and it will automatically be downloaded and updated on all other Dropbox computers you own.

Using other operating systems is not complicated when you connect them together. So long as the computers are on the same network you can create file shares, join them into a domain, or use a simple service such as Dropbox.

Useful Applications

Here is a list of the best Applications for your Ubuntu system that will help you get the most out of your computer.

- Office Productivity – Abiword, VI, Emacs, LibreOffice, nano

- Multimedia – VLC, DeaDBeef, Cmus, AquaLung, MPlayer, Miro

- Web Browsing – Firefox, Chromium, Midori, W3M

- Creativity – Aud

- acity, GIMP

- Other – Kupfer, Thunderbird, qBittorrent

And for programs that help with usability, there are so many varied choices that it depends on what you are trying to accomplish. The best way to discover a program is to search on the internet for a functionality you wish to add. For example, if you are searching for a quick way to open and close the terminal you might come across the program "Guake". Or if you are wanting audio within the terminal it might recommend "Cmus". Finding the perfect applications for you is part of the customization aspect of Linux, and it makes every install a little more personal for each user.

Administration

If you are looking for a "Control Panel" of sorts, you can find shortcuts to administrative tools such as network, printing, keyboard, appearance, and more from within the "System Settings" application. Some Ubuntu variants use "Settings Manager" or just "Settings" for the same purpose.

After launching it there will be links to other default configuration applications; just click on whichever you need to change to obtain a GUI for settings a few options. But not everything administrative is found through the GUI. Most low-level settings are only available through the command line, and as such you will need to know exactly what to type to edit them.

As an example, adding a new user to Ubuntu requires the "adduser" command. By following the command with a username, the terminal will prompt for basic information and a password. Setting that new user to be an administrator is done with "usermod -aG sudo nameofuser". Moreover a user can be deleted with "deluser". These options are difficult to find through GUI but can be done in seconds with a terminal.

"Task Manager", or the administration of running applications within Ubuntu is done through the terminal as well. The program "top" is standardly installed on all distributions (mostly), and starting it displays a list of all currently running processes as per task manager. By default though, the list of processes will be updated and moving around in such a way that it might be difficult to read the data we need. Press the "f" button to bring up a sorting list, navigate to "PID" with the arrow keys and press "s" to set over that option. Now use escape to return to top and we can now scroll through the list with page-up and page-down to view the tasks. Say, for instance, we want to close the program

"Pidgin" because it is unresponsive. Find it in the list (or search for it with the above filtering commands) and take note of the PID (Process ID) number. Press "q" to quit top, then type "kill 4653" obviously replacing the number with the PID. At any time within top you can press "h" to see a list of keyboard shortcuts for various actions. If top is too difficult to use consider installing "htop", a "human readable" version of the program. It actually shows neat ASCII graphs detailing CPU, RAM, and other usage statistics. Search for a program with F3, then use F9 and Enter to kill it.

As for services, you might have noticed we use the "service" command to change their status. So starting a web server would be done with "service apache2 start", restarting it done by replacing start with restart, and stopping it by replacing start with stop. Finding a list of services is done with "service --status-all". Services are daemons, or background tasks that are continuously running. They can be gathering data, running a service such as Bluetooth and Wi-Fi, or waiting for user interaction.

Security Protocols

Linux has a focus on security in general, which contributes to its use in corporate and server settings. Taking advantage of the security protocols means that you are more secure than other operating systems and less likely to have your computer compromised. This requires good security principals, of course, and always being safe online. A computer without a password is hardly protected at all.

One feature brought over from UNIX is file permissions. Every file has a set of permission- the owner, group, and rights. The command "chown" changes the owner of a file, "chgrp" changes the group, and "chmod" changes the rights associated with the file. Discovering the permissions of a file or folder is done by typing "ls -l filename". It will return an initially confusing line such as "- rw- rw- r--". "R" means read, "W" stands for write, and the third option is "X" for execute.

The three sets are respectively owner, group, and other. So our example file above has read and write permissions set for the owner and its group, but only read permissions for other users. This means that the owner and the group he belongs to (most likely sudo users) have permission to both access the file and change its contents, but other users on the network or PC can only view the contents and not edit it. Script files will need to have the X in order to be executed, and without it they cannot be run.

Most people will only need to use the "chmod" command to change the permissions of files they wish to use. We use the command and a set of numbers to set the permission of the file. "chmod 777 test.sh" makes the file readable, writable, and executable by all users anywhere because each specification (owner, group, other) has the number 7 attached to it. Numbers determine the permissions that entity has, and the number used is calculated like so:

- Start with the number 0.

- Add 4 for adding readability.

- Add 2 for write-ability.

- Add 1 for executable-ness.

- The number you have left determines the permissions.

6 would be read/write, but 1 would only be executable. 5 would be readable and executable, but not changeable. In our 777 example, we set owner, group, and others to all be 7. This is not particularly good security, because that means anybody anywhere can mess with that file. A more conservative permission set would be 775. Use security permissions advantageously for secure computing.

Security within Linux expands beyond just permissions. Ensure that you practice good security practices, and that you are following common sense in regards to security- install

only needed programs, do not follow all
internet advice, do not use sudo too often, use
passwords, use encrypted networks, keep
software up to date, encrypt important files,
and make regular backups. As a final word of
advice, look into using a distribution with
SELinux, a module that supports AC and
other security policies.

Scripting

Bash is the "programming language" or the terminal. When we type a command, we are doing so within bash. A script is a list of bash commands that execute in order, meaning we can create a script with a list of commands and run it to save time or automate terminal tasks that we normally have to type. As an intermediate and advanced Linux administrator, you can use scripts to greatly shorten the amount of work required for repetitive or constantly running tasks.

To start a script, create a new file "script.sh" within nano. The first line must always be "#!/bin/bash" to mark it as a bash script. Type the following lines for your first script.

echo "What is your name?"

```
read name
```

```
echo "Hey, $name. Here is your current
directory, followed by the files."
```

```
Pwd
```

```
Ls
```

Save the script. Now we have to set the permissions to allow it to be run. Use "sudo chmod 777 script.sh", and then run the script with "./script.sh". So long as you copied the script exactly, it will ask for your name and then show you your directory and files. Take the concept and expand it further in your own scripts. You can run commands from installed programs as well, so you can write a script that automatically joins a domain, or one that connects to the network specified. Shutting down remote computers is a great automatic task as well.

Scripts can either be run manually or set to execute at certain times. To run a certain script every time the user logs in, open the "startup applications" program from dash and create a new app with the script as the source. Now every time that user logs in the script will run automatically. This is useful for setting up certain options or starting background services without requiring the user to do it themselves.

Scheduling tasks for a certain time can be done with the Cron system daemon. It is installed be default on some systems, but if not "sudo apt-get install cron" can be used. Start the service with "service cron start" and create a new crontab file with "crontab -e".

Select nano as your text editor. At the bottom of the created file, add a new line with our scheduled task. The format goes as follows:

minute, hour, day, month, weekday, command

And we format it with these options to specify when to run the command. Time numbers start with 0, so the hours range from 0 to 23 and minutes are from 0 to 59. Replace any option with an asterick to specify that it will run on any value. Pay attention to these examples:

0 12 * * * ~/script.sh

This will run the script.sh found in the Home directory every day at noon.

30 18 25 12 * /usr/bin/scripts/test.sh

And this will run test.sh within the /usr/bin/scripts directory at 6:30 on Christmas day every year.

Conclusively, scripting and automating scripts are fantastic ways to take administrative control of regularly occurring tasks. Continue writing scripts, or look up examples online to see how your computing experience can be made easier with bash.

Advanced Terminal Concepts

Mastering Linux comes down to intimate comprehension of the tools available in the OS and how to utilize them. Many of the topics discussed in this chapter will focus on more tasks and how to accomplish them, or a few QOL improvements to the OS in general.

Compression and decompression of files often confuses Linux beginners. The tools are typically already installed, but the command line must be used. Furthermore, the strange .tar and .gz file-types are Linux-specific formats that you might often come across. All files can be unzipped or zipped with the gzip tool. Preinstalled on Ubuntu, we access it with the "tar" command. To compress a folder and the files contained within, navigate to it in terminal and type "tar –czvf name.tar.gz foldername". C stands for "create", z means "compress (gzip)", v is for "verbose", and f allows filename specification. If you want more compression (but at the cost of time), zip the folder with gzip2 by replacing the –z switch with the –j switch instead.

Now extracting that same archive can be done with "tar –xzvf name.tar.gz". You will notice that the –c was replaced with an –x, and this indicates extraction. Once again if you are dealing with bzip2 files use the –j switch instead.

Continuing with advanced terminal concepts, let us talk about a few quality tips and tricks that can save you time in the terminal. When typing a command or file name, press tab halfway through. This feature, tab completion, will guess what you are attempting to type and fill in the rest of the phrase. For files it will complete the name as shown in the directory, or complete a command by considering what you are trying to do. Linux experts and anyone that has to use the terminal regularly may seem as though they are typing exactly what they want with extreme accuracy and speed, but they are actually just using tab completion.

Users, especially administrators, will spend a decent amount of time with the sudo command because their instructions require elevated privileges to run. But when typing out a long command and forgetting to type sudo, you will be angered at having to type it again. Instead simply type "sudo !!", shorthand for "super user do again". It generously saves from typing an entire command again.

Another method of repeating commands is to use the up and down arrows. Pressing up continuously cycles through previously typed commands. You can also edit the commands with the left and right arrows to change the text contained within.

And the most requested terminal tip involves copy and pasting. Attempting to paste a line into the terminal results in the strange character ^v. The keyboard shortcut is not configured to work in the terminal, and that is why the strange combination is displayed. To actually paste, right click and select the option; or use the key combination shift+insert. Copy in the same way, but with ctrl+insert instead. While it might be okay to copy and paste terminal commands from the Internet (provided you understand the risk and know what they are doing in the command), do not try to paste from this publication. The formatting introduced through the medium in which you are reading it might have inserted special characters that are not recognized by the terminal, so it is best if you do not copy and paste, but rather you should type manually any commands presented.

Linux has a hidden feature that not many users know about. Files are displayed to the user when you visit that directory or type ls, but actually not all of the files are viewable this way. In Linux if you name a file with a period as the first character it will be marked as hidden. Hidden files are not normally visible by common users, and it acts as a way to protect configuration files from accidental editing/deleting/so forth. To see those files, we only need to add the −a tag to our ls search. In the GUI press ctrl+h in a directory to reveal the secret content. And as you create scripts and other configuration files consider hiding them with the period as a form of user protection.

Any command within terminal can be interrupted or quit with the ctrl+d key combination. Use it to stop a lengthy process or to exit out of a program/command that you do not understand.

Aliasing is a way to create your own personal shortcuts within the terminal. Instead of typing a long command or a bunch of smaller commands aliases can be used to combine them into a single user defined option. Just as the name implies, aliases are different names for anything you specify. Every alias is contained within a hidden config file- begin editing it with "nano ~/.bashrc". Because it exists within the user's home directory every alias will be pertinent only to that user. At the bottom of the file we can begin creating alias as per the following example:

alias gohome='cd ~ && ls'

This alias will change the directory to home and display the contents by typing "gohome". When creating aliases you must follow the formatting presented above exactly, meaning there is no space between the command and the equal sign. Multiple commands are strung together inside the single quotes separated by "&&". For more robust aliases, add a function instead. The following example combines cd and ls into a single command.

```
function cdls () {


    cd "$@" && ls
}
```

 After writing your aliases, save the file and restart the computer. Your new commands are then available for use.

 That file we edit, .bashrc, is the configuration file for the Ubuntu terminal. Besides making aliases we can also use it to customize our terminal settings, such as color, size, etc... A quick tip is to uncomment the "#force_color_prompt=yes" by removing the # and ensuring "yes" is after the equals. This adds color to the terminal, making certain words different colors. More options are available when you open a terminal, right click on it, and select profiles followed by profile preferences. Through the tabs here you can customize the font, size, colors, background colors, and much more. Customization of the terminal is recommended if you are going to be using it a lot, because it helps to be comfortable with the tools you will work with.

I/O Redirection

During normal terminal command execution, "normal input" (typed by the user, or read from a file/attribute/hardware) is entered and parsed by the command. Sometimes the command has "standard output" as well, which is the return text shown in the terminal. In "ls", the standard input is the current working directory, and the standard output is the contents of the folder.

Input and output are normally direct, but by using I/O redirection we can do more with the terminal. As an example, the "cat" command (concatenate) followed by a file will output that file to the screen. Running cat by itself opens a parser where any line that is input will be immediately output (use ctrl+d) to quit. But with I/O redirection hotkeys (<, >, <<, >>, |) we can redirect the output to another source, such as a file. And "cat > test.txt" will now put the standard output in that new file. Double signs signify appending, so "cat >> test.txt" will place the output at the end of the file rather than erasing the contents at the beginning.

The vertical line character, or the "pipe", uses another form of I/O redirection to take the output of one command and directly insert it into the input of another. "ls | sort −r" would take the output of ls and sort it into a backwards list. We redirected the output and gave it to another command to accomplish this.

And finally, the "grep" command is used very often within I/O redirection. Grep can search for a certain string within a specified file and return the results to standard output. Using redirection, this output can be put into other commands. An interesting feature of Linux to note is that object is a file, even hardware. So our CPU is actually a file that stores relevant data inside of it, and we can use grep and other tools to search within it.

That example is fairly advanced, but here is a simpler instance:

"grep Conclusion report.txt"

And it will search within the file for that specific word. I/O redirection can become a complicated process with all of the new symbols and commands, but it is a feature that you can incorporate into your scripts and daily use that often allows for certain features and functions of Linux to be done in a single line.

Linux and the terminal are difficult concepts to fully master. But with practice and continuing dedication you will be able to perform masterful feats of computing and do helpful tasks that are not possible in Windows or OSX. Learning more about commands and how to use them certainly helps in this regard, so persist in your studies of new commands and their use. Positively the only command you actually need to memorize is "man", a command that will show the manual pages and documentation of any other command specified. The manual pages show switches, examples, and the intended use of every command on your system. Use the tool to your advantage and gain intimate knowledge of your system.

More Linux Information

To continue learning about Linux and the possibilities it can provide, consider the examples in this section. It will briefly discuss more uses for Linux, and a few other concepts that have yet to be talked about.

The "Linux file system" refers to the main layout of the files and folders on your computer. If you continue to "cd .." in the terminal, or if you click the back button on the GUI until it goes no further you will stumble upon the "root" directory. The folders here, bin, boot, etc, usr, and so on are how your hardware and settings are configured. Each folder has a specific purpose and use, and you can understand them by exploring the contents. As an example, user data is stored in home, but user programs are stored in usr. Because of how diverse and complicated the file system actually is it will not be discussed here, but if you wish to learn more do an Internet search or read the documentation associated with your operating system.

Linux systems are often used for purposes other than desktop use. Dedicated machines run variants of Linux because of the power and stability it provides. Even our cars have a Linux kernel running to keep track of error codes and help mechanics.

Servers often have Linux installed because of reliability and the functions the distributions have within them. For instance, Linux machines are used as firewalls because the "iptables" application provides excellent port blocking and intelligent filtering. You yourself can run a firewall on your system with the application as well, thus gaining business-level software for free. In this way, Linux is also great for networking. The machine can act as a switch, router, DNS server, DHCP server, and more just by installing the relevant applications.

And finally, Linux systems are not limited to the interfaces we have seen insofar. Every distro has its preferred desktop environment, but the interface can be extremely customized to the individual's preference. There are even file and web browsers for the terminal, which is greatly helpful for those using SSH or remote computing. All-in-all, you should try out different DE's by installing them and configuring them to your liking.

What Next and Conclusion

How you continue depends on what you want to do with your Linux distribution. For casual browsing and simple use, continue with Ubuntu and install the programs you need. For more adventurous people, consider installing a new distribution to see what each has to offer. Those wishing to learn even more deeply about Linux can install one such as Arch or DSL to build their own unique OS from scratch. Administrators and power users can install a server version of a distro to build their own Linux network, or they can consider changing over their environment from other operating systems to entirely free ones.

Conclusively, Linux is a powerful and relatively easy to use set of operating systems. But their real potential comes from the hard-to-master terminal and command line functions. Thank you for reading this publication, and I hope that it has shed some light on the mysterious subject of the defacto alternative operating system. If Linux has confused you or did not live up to expectations, I implore you to take a second look at the features it can offer. While it may not have the same caliber of games or 3rd party proprietary software, the OS is simple and customizable enough to be used as a primary OS with maybe Windows or OSX as a secondary OS. Alternatives exist for just about every program, so if it is possible to get rid of Microsoft and Apple entirely, it is highly recommended you do so. Thank you again, and make good use of your new Linux knowledge.

Related Titles

Hacking University: Freshman Edition
Essential Beginner's Guide on How to
Become an Amateur Hacker

Hacking University: Sophomore Edition. Essential Guide to Take Your Hacking Skills to the Next Level. Hacking Mobile Devices, Tablets, Game Consoles, and Apps

Hacking University: Junior Edition. Learn
Python Computer Programming From
Scratch. Become a Python Zero to Hero. The
Ultimate Beginners Guide in Mastering the
Python Language

Hacking University: Graduation Edition. 4
Manuscripts (Computer, Mobile, Python, &
Linux). Hacking Computers, Mobile Devices,
Apps, Game Consoles and Learn Python &
Linux

Data Analytics: Practical Data Analysis and Statistical Guide to Transform and Evolve Any Business, Leveraging the power of Data Analytics, Data Science, and Predictive Analytics for Beginners

About the Author

Isaac D. Cody is a proud, savvy, and ethical hacker from New York City. After receiving a Bachelors of Science at Syracuse University, Isaac now works for a mid-size Informational Technology Firm in the heart of NYC. He aspires to work for the United States government as a security hacker, but also loves teaching others about the future of technology. Isaac firmly believes that the future will heavily rely computer "geeks" for both security and the successes of companies and future jobs alike. In his spare time, he loves to analyze and scrutinize everything about the game of basketball.

www.ingramcontent.com/pod-product-compliance
Lightning Source LLC
LaVergne TN
LVHW052307060326
832902LV00021B/3748